Girl Talk

Poetic Reflections of Self-Esteem, Self-Acceptance, Self-Respect and Faith.

Girl Talk

Charmaine Galloway

www.charmainegalloway.com

ISBN 13:978-0615945187

ISBN 10061594518x

Library of Congress Control Number: 2013923667

Printed in the U.S.

Cover Design by AP Designz

Grammatical Editing by Felicia Thomas and Epic Kreationz

Contact the author by email: mscharmgall@yahoo.com

Dedication

This book is dedicated to all the girls around the world
Girl you rock
Therefore, don't let anyone tell you differently
Shine bright like a diamond
Because *you* are amazing.

For Shayla

Table of Contents

Table of Contents

Part One

Girl Power

For you created my inmost being; you knit me together in my mother's womb. I praise you because I am fearfully and wonderfully made; your works are wonderful,
I know that full well.
Psalm 139:13-14

Girl U Rock

You encourage yourself to stay positive
You know your self-worth and
You put God first
Girl you rock!

You live your life to the fullest and you reach for the stars
You surround yourself with positive folks who know that wisdom and prosperity will take you far

When you are lonely
You know that you are truly not alone,
Because God will never leave your side.
In Him, you can confide in
Believe in God's word and you will always win
Girl you rock!

You stay focused on continuing your education
You know that the more you know
Your comprehension grows and you can impact the nation
Girl you rock!

You rock because you believe that God is your refuge and strength
He is ultimate security
With Him you shall never flee
Girl you rock!

You rock because you know not to fall for the sins of the world
People look at you and they see that you're no ordinary girl
You are a child of God
You are delighted to be on God's team
You are blessed and highly favored because you rock with the King

The Devil prowls around like a roaring lion, seeking people to devour
You rock because no weapon formed against you shall prosper;
You are more than a conqueror
When you come across situations that aren't right
You know when it's time to take a hike
Girl you rock!

On days when you don't feel that you rock
You get on your knees and pray to the Lord to give you strength and the confidence that you need

Everyone goes through trouble in their lives
But all you need to do is dust off and walk with great stride.
Next time you won't go that route
Because now you know what's best
And God puts everyone through a test

You know when to move on and let go of the past
Because you know that trouble doesn't always last
Keep your head up and succeed to the next task because
Girl you rock!

Life don't stand still.
Stand strong and depend on God's will
The devil will try to destroy and kill
But you don't put up a fight because you know God is real
What did God say to do when times are hectic. "*Be Still.*"

He lives in those who believe
Just trust in Him and His grace and mercy are what you will receive.
Girl you rock!
So rock on with your blessed self.

Beautiful

You need to always know
That you are beautiful

When your hair is curly
or if you wear it straight
or even if you rock it natural
Baby girl, you are beautiful

If you are thin and tall
or even thick and small
Baby girl, you are beautiful

No matter what your complexion is
Never wear a frown
Be confident in the skin you're in
If anyone ever tries to check you about your beauty
Let them know that God has created you perfectly

You don't need anyone to validate your beauty
Because you know how to praise yourself

Every morning when you rise
Look in the mirror and say
"I am beautiful in every way."

You may not have everything you want
But God provides you with everything you need
Pick out your clothes for the day
Get dressed, look in the mirror and say
"I look great today."

You need to always know
You are beautiful in every way

Love yourself
Respect yourself
Despite what others may say

This Is Who I Am

Girls say:
I am a **winner** and I will not stop running until I win the race
I am a **warrior** no matter what challenges I face
I am **strong**
I am a **believer**, so when I feel weak, God will give me the strength to carry on
I am **smart** and I want to be successful
I am **striving** for my future
I am **comfortable** even when it thunders and rains
I am **confident** that God will stop the storm and relieve my pain
I am **vocal**
I am **free** to speak up for myself
I will not allow anyone to make a servant out of me
I am **worthy** of the best
I am **certain** that I will not settle for anything less than the best
I am a **leader** and when I see my peers doing wrong, I will not follow
I am **sure** that I will turn away from relationships that are hollow
I am **talented** and I have many skills
I am **someone** who will use my gifts to serve God's will
I am **optimistic** that whatever God has for me is for me
I am **blessed** to know that I was put on this earth to fulfill my destiny
I am
I am
Whatever I believe and speak out of my mouth.

Charmaine Galloway

Hello Fear

Fear, why do I listen to you?

I do know that God didn't give me a spirit of fear.

So why do I trust in you?

My heart is broken because of you.

Don't you freight or fear

God is able and He is sincere.

We all may worry sometimes

Think positive and leave your past behind.

Don't be timid, Don't be weary, Don't give up

The sky is the limit.

So dry your tears and pray to God

He will free you from your fears.

Hello fear, I will no longer allow you to

Hold me back from my hopes and dreams.

I am no longer afraid

Because I live for the King.

My heart is no longer your home

Good-bye fear, I am letting you go and now I am free

You will no longer have control over me.

Charmaine Galloway

Never Give Up On Your Education

Your teenage years and school days
Will never reappear
So make the best out of this time in your life
Do what is right
Keep your eyes on the prize
Don't limit yourself; keep your head up and rise
Rise over every obstacle that tries to block your vision
You have the power to make great decisions
Do the best you can
Don't settle for average
Go above and beyond
When people say you can't
Push harder and prove them wrong
Don't stop at a High School Diploma
Get your college degree
Show others that you are smart and intelligent
And that you handle your responsibilities
They will see
That you are moving closer to becoming the Queen
That God had created you to be
The devil wants to see you fall
But rebuke him in the name of Jesus and stand tall
Follow your dreams
Sometimes it may get tough
Ask God for strength
With Him you can accomplish anything
Just remember God has a plan for you
You were put on this earth for a reason
Keep your head up and put up a fight
So you can live an abundant life
This may be your season.

Girls, Girls, Girls

So I guess you think you grown

News flash…

You are not grown

Not until you are eighteen and out of my home.

So lose the attitude

Because it's not cute

And it's very rude.

When you're being disrespectful

Don't expect me to be graceful.

You will still follow my rules

And perform well in school.

Enjoy your young years

Have all the fun that you can.

Don't rush to become grown

You will have so many responsibilities

When you are old enough to be on your own.

So now let me teach you the facts of life

So when that time comes

You will be ready and you won't lose sight.

I've been your age before

And I know all teens want to explore

Different things in the world

But there is so much negativity going on

I am just trying to teach you and get you ready

Before you walk out the door.

I am your caretaker (mom, dad, grandparents).

Pay attention

When I talk to you and share information

That can help you

I only want the best for you

I love you and I hope you listen.

Celibacy

What is celibacy?

Keep reading and you will see.

Celibacy means not having sexual relations until you're married.

God made all girls pure

So never be unsure

When you are in doubt and you need to be reassured

Read God's word for guidance and strength

The best thing in your life is to be celibate.

Spend time alone to think and learn what you want in life

Keep the people that mean no good out of sight

Make responsible decisions and do what's right.

Part Two

Friends and Relationships

Do not be deceived: "Evil company corrupts good habits." 1 Corinthians 15:33

I Bet

You probably don't think that I am telling you the truth
When I say you are beautiful
You probably think that I don't understand what it is you're going through.

Because I am your mother/dad
And I am so much older than you
You probably think I'm not hip and know about the latest trends.

You may think I'm wrong
When I tell you that she isn't really a true friend
And that you are way too young to be thinking about having a boyfriend.

I know it can become overwhelming and sometimes you may be confused about the issues in life
But I am here to lead and help you do what's right.

When I was young, I went through some of the things that you may endure
But for your life I want so much more.

The years may have changed
But society is still the same
As it was when I was growing up
No it's not, now it's rougher.

I bet when you look back on life when you are older
You will say, "My mom was right, I should have listened to her."

Friends

What about your friends?

Some won't always be true

They may also turn their backs on you.

Love yourself enough to know

That without friends you can still grow

To become the person that God has created you to be.

It's okay to have a few

Maybe one or two

But it can get hectic

When you have too many people close to you.

That's when gossip will spread

When people begin to interfere

The trust has been broken and lies have been said.

Understand your value and self-worth

Don't be a follower

Be a leader and put yourself first.

Some girls can be so cruel

Bullying, teasing and fighting in school.

Those types aren't your friends

A true friend would never stab you in the back

They will always have your back

You should be able to confide in a true friend.

A true friend will respect you

Never neglect you.

They will talk to you when you are going through

A situation that has your mind baffled

They know that you would be there for them

If they needed you.

Choose your friends wisely

Make sure they are honest, confident

And that they have goals.

Don't hang around with foes.

Stay away from folks that are always negative and those who try to bring you down.

Those are not the ones you want to keep around

Hang with those who are on the path of accomplishing great things.

Those who are motivated to succeed.

So please be careful who you call your friends

Make sure they have your back in the end.

Boy Please

Boy please who are you trying to fool
Coming to her acting all cool
Can't you see
Your actions don't faze her
She's not trying to hear the gibberish that you speak
You're just like the others
Telling her that you will take care of her
But you still live with your mother

She is determined to be a Proverbs 31 woman
She will not focus on your mesmerizing eyes
And she will not fall for your lies.

Boy please your mind is so gone
She has a strong relationship with her heavenly father
And she makes sure that her mind doesn't roam.

She is not the type of girl
That would allow you in her world
To walk all over her
Then turn around and leave.

She has heard about you boys
The ones that always go astray
When you don't get your way.

The ones that kiss and tell
Then bail.

Try to run game on her it won't work
Because she knows her self worth

So don't try to label her as a girlfriend
She is a girl with high expectations

And she knows she has time to grow
While she waits for God to send her mate.

So for now, all that girlfriend, boyfriend talk can wait
Until God sends her mate.

She will let you know up front
That she is focused on her school work
And to better herself for what lies ahead in her life
She has no time for jerks.

So as soon as you come at her wrong
She will be long gone.

She is following the path that God has for her
She will not allow any mishaps to occur.

She will never allow anyone or anything
To stand in the way of spending time with her God
Boy please if you didn't know
You better wake up and see
That she is God's property.

Wrecking Ball

He was like a wrecking ball
He came in to her life
And when he left
He made her crumble and fall.

She trusted him
From the very start
But he turned on her
And broke her heart.

She felt like she would
Never get over the unbearable pain
It felt like she was going insane.

She tried to hide
The feelings she had inside
But she couldn't
Because she was dying inside
She cried and cried and cried.

She wanted to be strong and
Let go of him
Because she knew he was wrong
But she had no one to talk to.

She was told that relationships
Come and go
But she didn't know
That when it was over
She'd have a torn soul.

Part Three

Where is the Love

"For God so loved the world, that he gave his only Son, that whoever believes in Him should not perish but have eternal life John 3:16.

I Need Love

Who should I run to
When I am sad and blue?

Pray to the Lord our God
And He will see you through
The Lord hears your cries
He will never put more on you
Than you can bear
Call on Him and He will be there.

Sometimes it may seem like
He is not there when you call
Just remember He is always on time.
And He will not let you fall
Don't fear
Because He is always near.

Who's going to be there for me
When I feel alone and I'm lonely

When your friends and family walk away
Call on the Lord and by your side He will stay.
If you can't see your way out
He will guide you all the way.

But you have to take time out of your day
To read His word
Praise and worship His name
And Pray.

Run to the Lord when you need love.
Run to the Lord when you are confused
And don't know what to do.
Run to the Lord for all your needs.

But when things are great
Run to the Lord and praise Him
For His good deeds.

Jesus Love

Jesus love is unique
Jesus love is what you need
Pursue and you will see
That He is your everything.

Jesus love is pure
Love that you should adore
Love that you don't have to search hard for
Just read His word.

Jesus loves those who believe
That He died for you and me
On Calvary.

Now that love
Jesus love will never cease
Jesus love will endure and conquer anything.

I thank God that Jesus love will never terminate
For His name sake.

Yes, Jesus loves me
This I know
For the Bible tells me so.

Jesus love is enough to get you through
Your toughest struggles in life
From Him you do not have to hide
Oh how amazing, everlasting, and unconditional
Is Jesus love for us.

Charmaine Galloway

You Are My Everything

Lord I have loved you from the very start

Because you first loved me

We will never part

You are embedded in my heart.

I may have my family and friends in my crew

But no one will ever compare to you.

When I am lonely I can call on you

Your words of wisdom always guide me through.

I once was lost but know I am found

I can see that you always bring out the best in me.

Lord God, you are my everything.

Part Four

Corruption of the World

For all that is in the world, the lust of the flesh and the lust of the eyes and the boastful pride of life, is not from the Father, but is from the world.
I John 2:16

Charmaine Galloway

WWW Dot Com

Be careful what you post online
Your info will be spread like a drop of a dime.
Be mindful what words you spread around
Because online everything can be
Pulled up and found.
Don't share things that you will later regret
Don't post things that will make others upset.
Just remember before you download, press send,
Or post information that the world will see
Do things modestly and respectfully with integrity.
Don't expose yourself by taking pictures
Remember always be lady like and everything
Underneath your clothes should be out of sight
Once it's uploaded you cannot undo
So keep it simple and do what's right.
Don't trust people that you meet online
What they show and tell you can all be lies
Don't ever give
Your important information to people online
Because they can find you
And do things to you that are unkind.
Cyber bullying is so uncool

Bullying can cause you to be expelled from school.

Stay off Facebook, InstaGram,

Twitter and YouTube

If you are going to be disrespectful and rude.

Please keep it clean and be safe while you are on the world wide web.

Don’t act like fools because fools always lose.

Charmaine Galloway

It Could Have Been U

That could have been you
In that car that flipped over into the ditch
But God
That could have been you
In a homeless shelter with no family to take you in
But God
That could have been you
Used and abused with no way out of the situation.
But God
That could have been you
That lost a loved one and thought you couldn't go on without them.
But God.
It could have been you that thought you were
Too weak to stand
From all the pain and scars from your past
But God
But God
Means God loves you and He can and He is able
To pull you out of whatever you are going through
God knows your troubles and He will provide shelter, security and love to those that believe in His word.

Devil You Won't Keep Me in the Dark

You try to lend a hand
You say life is hard to understand.
I'm trying to find myself
But I don't know where to start looking
I try to carry the weight of life to keep me from sinking
But I only have two hands and they are becoming weak.
I'm trying to find my way through the darkness.
But I am so lost I wish I could see the light
I have lost focus and I need to get back on track
Of doing what's right
I wish I could wake up from this dark dream
This nightmare
Wait this can't be reality
I am losing focus on what is in front of me.
Devil you will not block my vision and try to steal my joy
Devil you are a lie
And you will not destroy me with this negativity.
Let me get on my knees and pray
To the Lord and He shall set my mind free.

Charmaine Galloway

Don't Get Lost in Society

Don't allow society to dictate who or what you are
Believe in your heart that you are a shining star
Don't do as you see on reality TV shows
Don't look at dancers from music videos as your role models.
You are beautifully created by God
Don't get lost in society
Society is filled with boys that will break you down
If you allow them to
Society is filled with alcohol and drugs
That will take over your mind, body and soul
Society is filled with so-called friends
Who don't care if you fall
Life is what you make it
Don't allow this world full of sin
To pull you in.

A Message to Young Girls

I wrote this poetry book for young girls and hoped that they would be able to visualize the significance of the poetry in their lives. As young people, we all go through different things in life. I hope that each girl that reads this book can take something from it that will better them in their life and bring them closer to our Heavenly Father.

Loving ourselves is one of the hardest things for many of us to do. As you ask the Lord to help bring balance into your life by placing Him first, He will help you nurture the most important areas of who you are. When negative thoughts, emotions or attitudes creep in, you need to turn your focus toward Jesus. Young girls, you were created by our Heavenly Father to do great and abundant things in life. Do not become bound by perceived expectations placed on you by parents, other family members, and friends or by pressures of society. Learn to see who you are, not as the world sees you, but as God sees you. It is hard to understand God's love for you until you appreciate who you are as a whole person. God created many facets of you, including the physical, spiritual, mental and emotional; coupled with the circumstances He sent to shape you, you are an amazing being to be loved.

Be mindful of the company you keep. Young girls, never allow people in your world who will try to pull you down. Stay focused on what God has for you and know that you do not have to settle for less with God on your side. If you are struggling with issues of life, please find someone you can talk to. Please, do not be afraid to ask for help if you need it. If you have been abused (sexually, verbally, physically or mentally), please seek help and inform someone that will help you heal from the abuse. Know that it was not your fault and you will feel better if you talk to someone about your pain; you can be set free.

Don't allow your mistakes and scars from your past to take over your future. Whatever you had done in the past is in the past. Start today by taking a new step forward into your future. Repent, ask God for forgiveness and don't look back. You may think that God will not forgive you of your sin. Yes, He can and He will. No matter the situation, God will bring you out and set your soul free. I am a witness. In my debut poetry book, titled My World, Through My Eyes, I shared, through poetry, my testimony of how God has kept me. In the next section of this book, I will share a few of those poems from that book. I *was* a lost soul. But God saved my soul and now I am a new person who lives for the King.

I hope that each girl who is touched by these poems will understand her Heavenly Father's unfathomable love for her and that her life has a divine purpose and value. Jesus Christ paid the price for us to have free and open access to God. If you are unsure about your relationship with Jesus, speak to your parents, a Christian friend or a pastor.

Blessings

Charmaine Galloway

Part Five

My World, Through My Eyes

Amazing Grace! How sweet the sound
that saved a wretch like me
I once was lost, but now I'm found
was blind, but now I see.

-John Newton

Charmaine Galloway

Prologue for
My World, Through My Eyes

My name is Charmaine, just a bony girl from Ohio. When I was young, I hated being skinny with a passion. I wanted curves and "meat on my bones" like the grown folks say. I allowed society to dictate to me what and who they thought I should be. But today, I know better.

I know who I am. I am a child of God. I now embrace and love myself the way God has created me. I know that He will carry me into my destiny and be with me as I fulfill my purpose. So you can like me as I am or, in the words of Martin Lawrence, "You can step!"

As a teen, I found joy in writing in my journal. It was therapeutic as it allowed me to escape from the negativity of my world. I wrote all of my thoughts, feelings, and emotions on paper. Having a positive outlet for my emotions and creativity encouraged me to see that there ***is*** positive light even within the hardships I have endured.

My brother and I were raised by our single parent mother. I was a young girl full of all kinds of negative emotions and insecurities, but I had goals and dreams. Throughout my life there were times I felt like giving up, as many of us do, but I didn't want to fail. Therefore, I pushed hard to succeed. With God's grace and mercy I have accomplished a lot that I am very proud of. One of those accomplishments that I am proud of is being first in my immediate family to receive my Bachelor's Degree. My life was not easy, but I'm blessed because it could have been much worse.

Most of the situations in this book are true stories I have gone through personally or have witnessed and held the hands of others close to me while they endured them. I'm sure many of you will be able to relate.

I believe that my purpose in life is to share my testimony of Faith. In this book, I will share one of the most valuable and essential lessons I have learned on my journey. Learning to Let Go and Let God intervene in my life and heal me from my sinful past has been the most life changing, validating, and peace yielding decision I have made for myself.

Right before I was about to send this book to be printed, I became so nervous. This is my truth, this is my story. The reason I wrote this book was to help young ladies understand that although they had a rough past, their future can be bright with the help of God. Author Essence M. Edward said to me, and I quote, "Once you sacrifice your work for others it's no longer your story". Her words helped me to let go of my fear, which has allowed me to share my world with you. The Lord has kept me and this is my testimony.

Are you ready to witness my world through my eyes? Well first, let me start at *the beginning*....(my teenage years)…

The Beginning: Lost Soul

"In the beginning it might be tough, put up a fight and don't give up".
-Charmaine Galloway-

Poetry

I've opened up to you daily,
You saved me.

I've expressed my emotions,
I've shared my feelings,
You were my daily devotion.

I painted a picture,
It made my soul richer.

Writing allows me to express how I feel.
Everything I write is real.

Life can be tough,
I write because I want to inspire others
To never give up.

Poetry was the key
That unlocked the pain that was inside of me.
And now my soul has been set free,
All because of my poetry.

Now I Rise!
Because you will see
My world through my eyes.

Charmaine Galloway

Caution: Do Not Enter

My heart has been
Torn,
Hurt,
Broken,
Lied to,
Rejected
Through it all
You might not want to enter here
Because my heart has yet to heal

Lost Feelings

Sometimes I feel like I want to die inside,
It's an unfortunate feeling that I cannot hide.
I just want to be left alone and cry.

My mother said,*"It's ok to cry and to let it out,*
don't hold it in. If you have to, scream and shout!"

I feel lost, confused, and down.
The reasons for these feelings remain unfound.

I'm too young to be so depressed,
It often feels like my life is one big mess.
I often feel like giving up,
Seems like I never have any good luck.

Why do I feel this pain?
It's like a puzzle or a never ending game.
I have all the pieces and they appear to fit,
But the picture I see is definitely not legit.
I've asked myself many times, "Where do I go from here?
When will these feelings go away, when will they all begin to disappear?

You....

I trusted you.
You betrayed me.
How could you?
Why would you
Tell people
What I told you?

I would never
Tell people what
You have confessed to me.
You are so fake.
You just couldn't wait
To open your mouth.

How sad.
But I'm not mad.
I just don't understand.
Maybe it's not meant
For me to understand.

You don't have to worry
About me coming to you,
Confiding in you
Ever Again
You so-called friend.

Insecure

Girl Talk

Sometimes I don't feel pretty.
I think I'm way too skinny.

I feel like I don't belong.
I feel all alone.

Sometimes I'm scared
I feel no one cares

I'm filled with pain
Am I insane?

Insecurity
Pain
Please go away!

Charmaine Galloway

Need to Find My Happy

Sorry if you're looking
For a happy poem
Since most of my poetry
Flows to a sad tone.
It's just another sad love song.
You know the songs
That Mary J. Blige sang
Until she found love.

I want to paint a picture with words,
Of the feeling that you get
When you see a beautiful white dove
Being set free
To fly high
In the sky.

Hold up one second,
Let me think
Of a joyful line.
Damn it seems like
Nothing fitting comes to mind.
To be continued

My prayer for the Lost Souls

Lord thank you for healing my soul. I know that I don't have the power to change myself, but I believe that You will change me as I trust in you. So Lord for those people that have hatred, hopelessness, and insecurity in their hearts, Lord I ask you to touch them and let them know that those emotions are not of you. Lord today I pray that You heal all of the "Lost Souls". Lord when they are down and out my prayer is that they seek your word which will reveal to them that there is hope for the hopeless and the hurting. And there is love that will out weight the hatred that is in their hearts.

Where's the Love

"Love comes from within. Seek and find Gods love first, before you try to love someone".
-Charmaine Galloway-

Love

Love is beautiful,
Like a garden full of roses.
Love is sweet,
Like a cold glass of lemonade
On a hot summer day.
Love can make you cry,
Love can make you smile.
Love is being honest,
Love is Powerful,
Understanding,
Compromising.
Love is being faithful,
Love is enduring,
Love is being respectful.
Love is unique,
Love is hard to keep.
Love is not perfect,
Love is not easy.
Love is passionate,
Romantic.
Love hurts.
Love heals.
Love is being real.

Charmaine Galloway

Teenage Love

It was love at first sight.
When we met he asked me,
Was I sure that I was ready
To be in a committed relationship.
I said yes, 'cause I thought I was.
My mother had a fit
Because he was nineteen and I was sixteen.
She wanted to make sure that his
Feelings were legit
And that I wasn't just some random chick.
He was always true,
He taught me how to love,
He showed me what it felt like to be loved.
After three years we grew apart
Because I was too young to understand
How to be with a real man.
A mature man that took care of his responsibilities
Like a man should.
I was a teenager

And I wanted to do all of the things that teenagers did.

I didn't know any other way,

So unfortunately I let him slip away.

A couple of years ago he passed away

Due to health issues.

"Darn I miss you."

It's sad to say

I have not run across anyone quite like him.

I long to find true love like that again one day.

Rest in peace to the teenage love I lost,

But you will always be in my heart.

Charmaine Galloway

God Sent

My belly aches
Wondering when will I find
That special mate.
It's been a long wait,
How long will it take?
I don't know,
But I will continually walk in faith.

I pray
And then I wait.
I do what the Lord says,
I will take it day by day.
I do not need any more heart breaks.

God knows I can't take any more for goodness sake.
God, I will patiently wait
For You to send me down
The right path to the golden gate.
When I open the gate there will stand my mate.

My prayer for LOVE

Lord, I have not found true love yet and I am not worried because I trust in You. I am in no rush to start another unhealthy relationship, that is why I am waiting on You. I know when the time is right and when my heart is fully prepared for love, You will send me the God fearing man that I have been praying for. Lord, I ask that You heal the tainted love that some share and bless them with Your almighty love. I pray that they seek You before they seek love from man. You are God and God is Love. Amen.

Unbreakable

"Love, respect, and encourage your family members. You must forgive the ones who hurt you, pray for them and move on. Family should be unbreakable.
-Charmaine Galloway-

Dear Momma

We have come a long way baby!
You have raised me
To become a strong and intelligent lady.
The journey was not easy,
But it could have been worse.
With all due respect, my thanks go to God first.
I sometimes reminisce on my childhood,
You were a single parent raising my brother and I.
We were raised in the hood,
I know you did what you could.
That is what made me strong,
As a child I didn't want to do wrong.
I saw you and my brother go through a lot of pain,
I tried to stay sane,
I did not complain.
My brother was affiliated with gangs
And he was always running away from home.
While he was out in the streets doing wrong,
I had heavy issues of my own.
We moved to many different homes,
I had to change schools,
For me that wasn't cool.
I was shy,
It took some time
For me to adjust and unwind.
I wasn't getting much attention at home,
So I begin sneaking and doing things on my own.
I remember whenever I felt low
You told me I was beautiful.
Yet, I didn't believe you
Because when I looked in the mirror
Beauty, I did not see.
I wanted to be pretty just like you,

You were so beautiful to me.
But mom things are better than they were before,
You have been my rock,
I couldn't ask for anything more.
When I need you, you are always here to listen.
Now you give me your undivided attention.
Did I forget to mention?
That whenever I thought I could not make it through
I would pick up the phone and call you.
We would pray together,
You would tell me things would get better.
We would talk on the phone all night,
You would not hang up the phone
Until you knew I was alright.
Now you have a granddaughter that adores you,
She is proud and knows that she is your boo.
I wouldn't change anything
Because my past is what has made me
The go-getter that I am today.
You have paved the way
For me to have a brighter day.
Our sky is no longer gray.
God has good plans for us,
As long as we have faith and pray
I believe everything will be ok.
We have come a long way baby!
Life is a journey and we're making it
I just wanted you to know that you are appreciated.

Daddy

Daddy, my world was so blue.
Where were you, when I needed you?
Why weren't you ever around?
My whole world was upside down.
All I wanted was for you to be my backbone
When I was too weak to stand.
When I was scared,
I wanted you there to hold my hand.
I wanted you to hold me
And tell me, that you would be there always.
I wish you would have taught me
How to handle situations when things got rough.
Why weren't you there when times were tough?
When life wasn't fair
Why weren't you there
To give me your all,
There to pick me up whenever I'd fall?

Daddy, Daddy, I needed you!

Daddy, my heart ached for you to love me.
I always wanted to be daddy's little girl,
It would have been wonderful
To have my daddy in my world.
Daddy why weren't you there?
To tell me that I was your beautiful little daughter?
I needed that love and encouragement from my father.
Come to me and hug me tight
And tell me everything would be alright.
Daddy, tell me I no longer have to fight,
Fight for you to notice me.
I tried to cope,

I cried out for hope.
All I wanted was for you to support me,
It felt like you aborted me.

Now I am grown
With two children of my own.
Daddy, we are building a relationship,
But we still have issues to resolve.
Thanks for being there when I call.
Thank you Lord
For healing my broken heart
And for giving my daddy and I
A brand new start.

Daddy, I love you.

Stepfather

He told me he was there if I needed him to be.
He was there to share my accomplishments in life,
He always told me he was proud of me.
At first it was hard for my brother and I to adjust
To a father figure in our home.
After a while we learned to love and respect him without a fuss.
We grew to know that, just like our mom, he only wanted the best for us.
My mom was delighted to be his wife
And we were content that he was in our life.
He was so happy when I had my first child,
He was ecstatic when he first held her in his arms.
The joy was on his face and in his smile.
When he met my male friends
He pointed out to me the ones that were up to no good,
But he also acknowledged the ones that were about something,
Who were on the right path of doing what they should.
It was hard growing up without my biological dad,
But after he came into my life I was no longer sad.
He was the positive male role model that I needed,
At that time of my life.
Thank you Step Dad.
I know he is in heaven watching over me,
He is no longer in pain now, he is resting in peace.

Charmaine Galloway

Little Brother

I know sometimes his life has been hard for him.
We grew up with no father,
So he didn't have a male role model.
I know that sometimes life can be unfair
Sometimes it seems like people just don't care.
I reminisce about our childhood,
I can remember he would always run the streets.
We were close when he was not out with his friends,
But not as close as I wish we could have been.
Even though I was older
He was always taller than me.
I looked up to him to protect me
And to be there when I needed him to be.
But sometimes when I needed him around
He was nowhere to be found.
"Life is hard but if you do the right thing
You will succeed
I pray that you just trust and believe
That you can do anything.
And believe what I say is true,
Lil Brother, I am always here for you and I love you."

If I Could

If I could
I would ease all the negatively in the world
So you will never have to sense it.

No hurt.
No worries.

No sadness,
No loneliness.

I wish I could block out all of these bad emotions
From entering into your life.
I wish I could be there beside you with every step you take.

But I can't.
But
God can and when you are going through
He will be there for you.

-Dedicated to my children-

Charmaine Galloway

I Need Your Attention

-Dedicated To Teenage Mothers-

Why won't you stop crying?
I changed your diaper.

Please stop crying,
I put you in the swing
You just screamin'.

What is wrong with you?
Are you sick?
Let me check your temp.

Stop crying, I am getting frustrated
What do you want?

Come here let me pick you up.

You stopped crying!

You just wanted me
To hold you,
To love you,
To look you in your eyes and talk to you

I Do Listen

Why do I fall so quickly?
When I fall why does it hurt so badly?
When I get up I find myself falling again,
Why don't men appreciate the woman that I am?
The woman that will be there,
The woman that always cares.
When situations go bad,
Why am I the only one so sad?
Why do I love so hard,
Only to be left scarred?
Why should I love again, to be treated wrong by these men?
Why do I give in?
I don't know why I rush
When I think things are good, my feelings get crushed.
Please help me out and tell me what I should do.

Sweetie, you need to ask yourself why do you fall so quickly.
You need to say no to John, Tom and Ricky.

Saying no is not easy,
No! I'm not sleazy,
But I like relations,
I know it takes time and patience.
How much time?
He takes me out and treats me so kind.

Honey, you need to take time to understand that man, Time to know his ways,
Just because he takes you out doesn't mean he's okay
Get to know his goals and his plans for the future,
Don't get involved with Jack,
If the only thing he owns is the clothes on his back.

Make sure he has a legal job, and don't still stay with his mother.
Do I need to go any further?

No, you can stop right there, I understand.
I **need** a man, why is it so hard for me to find a good man?

Listen sweetie,
Don't be so *needy*.
Most guys just want to play with your mind,
If he cares about you he won't mind waiting for the right time.
Stay out them clubs and go to church and pray,
Love yourself and God will send a good man your way.
Baby get yourself together,
Take your time, I promise things will get better.
You might fall again,
Call me whenever you need to talk,
Don't give in to these no good men.

Ok I am going to do what you say,
I'm going to be a stronger woman starting today.
I'm so happy I have you to talk to,
If it wasn't for you I don't know what I would do.

You always say that I don't listen to you,
Mom please believe
I do listen to you when you talk to me.

Family Gatherings

The ham is baking,
I smell Granny's yams.
The greens are cooking just right,
Such a beautiful sight.

The kitchen is overflowing with food
And scrumptious smells,
Just walking in the door
Puts you in a good mood.

Family talking
About the "olden' days",
Laughing,
Having a good time.

We hear a voice from the kitchen
"It's time to bless the food."
We all hold hands and pray,
Now it's time to eat,
There is nothing else to say.

Oh, what a sight!
At our family gatherings
This is what it's like.

.My prayer for Unbreakable Families

Lord I know that family is unbreakable, but I also know that we all have issues in our family that we need to pray on daily. Even though I had a rough childhood because of my parents' addictions, I love them both dearly. I am so thankful that they gave me life. I appreciate and learned so much from my life experiences. I am so blessed because I know my past situations could have been worse. Lord I thank you for my family. They are my blessings.

Lord, I pray that all the children that are raised in single parent homes receive the guidance that they need to be successful individuals in our society. Lord, I pray that they will rise above any bad situation in their lives. Amen.

Finding Myself

"This process was not easy, but when you put yourself first, learn to love yourself and call on God in your time of need. He will guide you in the direction you need to go to fulfill your destiny. This is my new beginning and God is in it."

-Charmaine Galloway-

I AM Nothing Without You

Lord, there is no one else like You,
There is no one that loves me like You do.
Lord, You are always here by my side,
From you there is nothing I can hide.
You are the step in my walk,
You are the sound
That comes out of my mouth when I talk.
You give me the energy that I have,
Lord, I love You with all my heart.
There is nothing in this world that will tear us apart.
Lord, it is You that I trust in,
You are my provider and my close friend.
The trust that I will not find in my family or friends.
You watch over me every day,
Your goodness and mercy guides me all the way.
Lord, at the end of the day I pray,
Knowing that You are looking over me.
It's You who wakes me up to see another day.
Lord, You are my heavenly father, my strength, and my salvation.
Lord, You are my everything without you I am nothing.

Cry No More

The little girl within me cries for love.
Lord, open my eyes so it's you I see
Because you love me unconditionally.
The little girl within me cries for guidance.
Lord, hold my hand and lead the way,
Reassure me that by my side
Is where you will stay.
The little girl within me cries for healing.
Lord, heal my pain and take away my worries made by man.
When I fall please take my hand.

*****

Little girl you are my child,
I will be there to wipe away your tears,
And I will take away your fears.
Love, guidance, and healing is what I have in store.
So little girl cry no more.

Charmaine Galloway

A Brand New Me

To the boys that call themselves men,
I'm not gonna worry,
I don't want to hear any more I'm sorry.
No more excuses,
No more lies.
Now I see what I didn't see before,
I do not need you to make me whole,
I will not let you hurt me anymore.
I'm moving on,
I want to be set free.
This is the brand new me.

For the chicks
That call themselves my so-called friends,
Where were you when I needed to talk?
Where were you during my celebrations?
My so-called friends were not at my graduations.
Why weren't you there to support me with my blessings?
I have learned a valued lesson.
You were not a true friend to me.
It's okay because I moving on,
I want to be set free,
This is the brand new me.

To my father,
I am your first born,
Without you my world was torn.
It took a long time for me to get to this point,
But I will no longer ask myself why.
I forgive you.
And I love you.
I just pray that you will stop letting the Devil win

And try to be the father that
You have not been.
I'm moving on from what happened in the past
I want to be set free
This is the brand new me.

To my Savior,
When my days are done here
I want to enter into Heavens gates.
I know You hold the key,
I will worship and praise your name faithfully.
This is the brand new me.
I know You will set me free.

I am not who I used to be
Can't you see.
I'm much stronger,
I'm much wiser.
I let go of my past,
I'm moving on.
I want to be free,
I found me,
I found my happy.

It's A New Day

I look back
At what I have been through over the years
And I can't help but to shed
Tears of joy because now I have the victory.
I have been through so much pain
And today I am sane.
It was my faith in God that
Turned my gray skies blue.
Today I am blessed and not stressed
About what tomorrow will bring
Because I now live only for the King.

No Regrets

I'm livin' my life,

I have always tried to do what's right,

But we sometimes lose sight.

Of course I've done some wrong on the way,

But today is a new day.

And I have no regrets.

I have no shame,

I'm glad I went through what I did

Because it made me a stronger woman.

I am willing to share

With others my past struggles

With insecurities and unhealthy relationships.

I don't mind sharing how I learned to put God first

And how I improved my self-esteem.

I have no regrets.

Survivor

I've watched,
Grown,
Learned,
Listened,
Disliked,
Loved,
Hurt,
Cried,
Lied,
Won,
Lost,
Given,
Taken,
Helped
Prayed
Survived.

After all I've been through
I stand strong,
I am a survivor
I did not do it on my own.
I never would have made it without God,
I would have lost my mind.
But I didn't because
God was there for me all the time.

The Best Things in Life are Free

They say that nothing in life is free
I beg to differ.
The best thing in life comes free to us,
Loving yourself and putting God first is a must
You may have to sacrifice other things in your life,
But living your life for Christ is Free.

Charmaine Galloway

Dream Seeker

I want to be a
Poet,
Author.
Motivational Speaker.

I want to be a
Business Owner,
Teacher,
Mentor,

I want to be a good
Mother,
Friend,
Wife.

But Lord, wherever I end up
I want to prevail.
I want to be remembered as someone
that has done well.

Ms. Independent

Since I've been grown
I've lived on my own.

What's the sense of renting a home
When I can have my own.

I am my own boss,
House note and car note
I'm paying them both off.

I pay my bills on time,
I work hard for mines,
I keep my money in line.

I'm a confident chick,
I make them haters sick.

I keep a job,
I don't answer to no man,
I depend on nobody,
I have an infinite plan.

Whatever I want to do, it's my choice,
I have my own voice.
I hope you don't get offended,
That's just me.
Ms. Independent.

Charmaine Galloway

Believe

They told me that life would be too hard
to live my dreams.

But,

I wanted to graduate from college,
So I did.

I wanted to buy a home
for my kids to grow up in,
So I did.

I wanted to run my own business,
So I did

I believed in myself
And now I'm following my dreams.

Secrets

There's no more secrets

I gave them all to you.

I don't want to act like

I'm living a perfect life

When my soul is dying inside,

Nowhere to run,

Nowhere to hide.

But You are my Father,

I have no secrets.

You already knew what I was going through

And that I needed you.

I just needed to surrender to you.

Charmaine Galloway

My Prayer

Lord, I once was lost but now I'm found. I was a lost soul. I praise your name for saving my soul and for allowing me to live an abundant life. I am nothing without You. When troubles surround me I will trust in you. Thank you for being there in my time of need. Even when I am unworthy you still perform miracles in my life.

My prayer is for those that are lost and think that their life is not worth living. Lord, I ask that you show up and show out in their lives. Those thoughts are of the devil and the devil is a liar. Bless them exceedingly and I pray that they let go and let God. Amen.

Corruption of the World

"The world we live in is full of sin. If you seek God's help in your endeavors, you will win."

-Charmaine Galloway-

Charmaine Galloway

Where I Come From

There are liquor stores on every other corner,
Homeless people walking the streets
Looking for change and food to eat.
Brotha's killing their brotha's,
Sistah's have no respect
For themselves or their mother.
Brotha's droppin' out of school,
No hope for attending college.
They think that hanging on the streets
And sellin' dope is cool.
Young girls trying their best
To provide for their one or two babies.
Mommy's baby.
Daddy's ?Maybe.
Minorities can't find good paying jobs,
So their next solution is to go out and rob.
They go into their neighbor's home
And steal their goods.
The cops never find the thieves
'Cause people don't snitch in the hood.
Where I come from.
People have to learn how
To survive the best way they can.
We can't do it on our own we need the Lord in our plans.

Killer

There is a killer on the loose,
He has killed a lot of folks.
He is attacking whoever comes close,
Please look out he is no joke.

It only takes him one night,
He will not let you out of his sight.
You might think I'm lying,
But everyday people are dying.

When he comes he will come out of nowhere,
He will attack women and men he doesn't care.
He is most wanted across the nation,
He doesn't care about the population.

He is fully loaded like a machine gun,
When he captures you, you can't run.
He is extremely dangerous,
He is undefeatable, every battle he has won.

When he finds you
There is nothing you can do,
Once you let him in there is no way out.
He will have you weak without a doubt.

The killer is AIDS

Yes, AIDS is killing a lot of people
AIDS is not curable, it is lethal.

Here are some healthy tips,
You don't have to have sex to be hip.

If you want to live long, do what's right,
Go get tested and live a healthy life.

Yes We Can

It is a new day,
History has been made.
An Afro-American man is our president,
He is God sent.
I never thought,
I never believed
That this would happen and I would be able to see.
That yes we can
Change the racial tension of Americans,
Yes we can
Make the United States a better place.
A black man ran and he won the race!
Yes we can
Be whatever we want to be.
Believing and having faith is the key.
Yes we can
One day see our children accomplish their goals
Yes we can
Help change our economy and make it safe for our children to grow.
Yes we can
Help Black men stay out of jail,.
Yes we can
Lower the rate of teen pregnancies
And lower the number of deadbeat dads in the city.
Let that young boy know he doesn't need to fight,
Let him know that killing his brother is not right.
Help that young girl build her self-esteem
And help every child live out their dreams.
We can do anything
As long as we believe
We will succeed.

We are living out Martin Luther King's Dream.
It took a long time,
But now it's our time to shine.
We will be strong and stand,
Every child, every woman and every man.
Yes we can!
Yes we can!
Yes we can!

Shy Girl

Hey why are you so shy?

Maybe because I don't want you to notice me,

Or maybe there is something about me that I don't want you to see.

Hey why don't you talk to anyone?

Maybe because I don't know what to say,

Or maybe I just don't know how to approach you in the right way.

Hey why are you always by yourself?

Maybe because I'm scared of what others will think of me.Is it me they want to be friends with or are they approaching me because I look lonely?

Hey why are you about to cry?

Maybe because I'm tired of feeling this way,

I wish I could wake up one day and everything would be okay.

No more insecurities,

No more low self-esteem,

And to have people look up to me.

By the way. Why are you asking me all these questions?

Because I used to be very shy,

I saw you sitting here alone and I wanted to say hi.

I also want to tell you that

I used to feel the same way that you do,

But God helped me and He pulled me through.

I stopped by to let you know

He can do the same thing for you,

Just trust in Him and your prayers will come true.

Fast Tail

Young girl you are not grown,
You need to slow your roll.
You are growing up too fast.
You need to wear clothes that cover your butt,
Hanging around a lot of boys is not very smart,
The way you dress and act
All they will do is break your heart.
Without all that make-up you are a pretty girl,
You better slow down
If you want to live long in this world.
A lot of bad things can happen these days,
You can get hurt, raped, or even catch AIDS.
You need to think about the things you do,
Your parents do not want
Anything bad to happen to you.
A beautiful princess is what they created,
So act that way, go to school and get educated.
You might as well enjoy your young life while you can,
Act like a child, you are not a grown woman.

My prayer for the corruption on the world

Lord, when I am oppressed, you hold me up. When I feel trapped in troublesome situations of the world you set me free. There is so much going on in this sinful world. I thank You for protecting me from harm and danger. I pray that others seek You when they need guidance, when they don't know where to turn. Lord, show us how to build one another up instead of knocking each other down. Lord, I ask that You shield us from negative influences and keep us from the temptations to do wrong. No matter what battles we are facing now or what might come in the future, God is on our side. And that means we can't lose.

About The Author

Charmaine was born and raised in Ohio. Writing has been her passion and a positive emotional outlet since middle school. As a teen, writing in her journal allowed her to escape from the negativity of her world. Around that time she also began writing her first fiction novel. She finds joy in creating unique and awe inspiring storylines for the characters in her stories. Creativity and imagination is a mainstay and compass in her work.

Charmaine has a Bachelor of Arts in Family Life Education and an Associate Degree in Early Childhood Education. Becoming a fierce advocate and supporter of troubled young women has been a goal of hers since overcoming struggles of her own as a young woman. "I believe turning a blind eye or deaf ear to our struggling youth only promotes destruction and demise. They are human. They have a voice. You'll be surprised by what you learn from them if you just listen."

Charmaine, being the wearer of many proverbial 'hats', is a self-publisher and founder of Charming Gal Publications. She is the CEO and jewelry designer for Forever Divas Fashionable Jewelry her online jewelry boutique.

The most important 'hat' she wears is being a Mom to her two children. Following her dreams as a writer, she is an authoress who will leave a beautiful legacy for them and encourage them to work hard to achieve their dreams because their Mom didn't quit reaching for hers.

Charmaine is currently working on new projects, so keep a look out for her upcoming releases. Please visit www.charmainegalloway.com to check out her blogs and new releases.

Please leave a review for this book on Amazon.com and GoodReads.com . I would love to hear your thoughts. Thanks for your support.

www.ingramcontent.com/pod-product-compliance
Lightning Source LLC
Chambersburg PA
CBHW060402050426
42449CB00009B/1866